This Reading Journal Belongs To:

Date

Published by Fairies and Fantasy Pty Ltd 2023

First Edition

Paperback ISBN: 978-1-922390-84-4

www.selinafenech.com

CONTENTS

Illustrated Bookshelf
1 .... TBR List
11 .... Read Again List
17 .... Recommendations
23 .... Loans In and Out
29 .... Book Reviews & Notes
132 .... About
137 .... Bookmarks

MY BOOKSHELF
~Write in the titles of books you've read~

MY BOOKSHELF
~Write in the titles of books you've read~

To Be Read

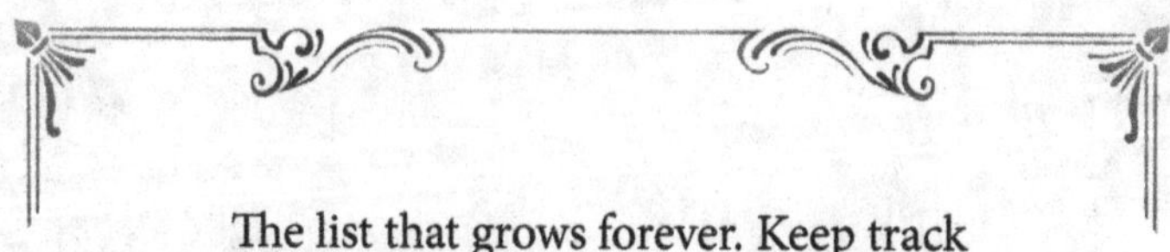

The list that grows forever. Keep track of the books you're planning to read and why you want to read them on the following pages.

TBR LIST

KEEP TRACK OF BOOKS TO BE READ.

TITLE AUTHOR READ? ☐

WHY?

TITLE AUTHOR READ? ☐

WHY?

TITLE AUTHOR READ? ☐

WHY?

TITLE AUTHOR READ? ☐

WHY?

TITLE AUTHOR READ? ☐

WHY?

TITLE AUTHOR READ? ☐

WHY?

TBR LIST

KEEP TRACK OF BOOKS TO BE READ.

TITLE AUTHOR READ?

WHY?

TITLE AUTHOR READ?

WHY?

TITLE AUTHOR READ?

WHY?

TITLE AUTHOR READ?

WHY?

TITLE AUTHOR READ?

WHY?

TITLE AUTHOR READ?

WHY?

TBR LIST

KEEP TRACK OF BOOKS TO BE READ.

TITLE AUTHOR READ? ☐

WHY?

TITLE AUTHOR READ? ☐

WHY?

TITLE AUTHOR READ? ☐

WHY?

TITLE AUTHOR READ? ☐

WHY?

TITLE AUTHOR READ? ☐

WHY?

TITLE AUTHOR READ? ☐

WHY?

TBR LIST

KEEP TRACK OF BOOKS TO BE READ.

TITLE AUTHOR READ? ☐

WHY?

TITLE AUTHOR READ? ☐

WHY?

TITLE AUTHOR READ? ☐

WHY?

TITLE AUTHOR READ? ☐

WHY?

TITLE AUTHOR READ? ☐

WHY?

TITLE AUTHOR READ? ☐

WHY?

TBR LIST

KEEP TRACK OF BOOKS TO BE READ.

TITLE AUTHOR READ? ☐

WHY?

TITLE AUTHOR READ? ☐

WHY?

TITLE AUTHOR READ? ☐

WHY?

TITLE AUTHOR READ? ☐

WHY?

TITLE AUTHOR READ? ☐

WHY?

TITLE AUTHOR READ? ☐

WHY?

TBR LIST

KEEP TRACK OF BOOKS TO BE READ.

TITLE AUTHOR READ? ☐

WHY?

TITLE AUTHOR READ? ☐

WHY?

TITLE AUTHOR READ? ☐

WHY?

TITLE AUTHOR READ? ☐

WHY?

TITLE AUTHOR READ? ☐

WHY?

TITLE AUTHOR READ? ☐

WHY?

TBR LIST

KEEP TRACK OF BOOKS TO BE READ.

TITLE AUTHOR READ? ☐

WHY?

TITLE AUTHOR READ? ☐

WHY?

TITLE AUTHOR READ? ☐

WHY?

TITLE AUTHOR READ? ☐

WHY?

TITLE AUTHOR READ? ☐

WHY?

TITLE AUTHOR READ? ☐

WHY?

TBR LIST

KEEP TRACK OF BOOKS TO BE READ.

TITLE AUTHOR READ?

WHY?

TITLE AUTHOR READ?

WHY?

TITLE AUTHOR READ?

WHY?

TITLE AUTHOR READ?

WHY?

TITLE AUTHOR READ?

WHY?

TITLE AUTHOR READ?

WHY?

Read Again List

Some books deserve another go around. Whether you want to relive the magic or need another look to better understand what was going on, create your read again list on the following pages.

Read Again List

List the books you loved so much you want to love them again!

Title

Author

Why?

Why?

Why?

Why?

Why?

Why?

Why?

LIST THE BOOKS YOU LOVED SO MUCH YOU WANT TO LOVE THEM AGAIN!

TITLE AUTHOR

WHY?

WHY?

WHY?

WHY?

WHY?

WHY?

WHY?

Read Again List

List the books you loved so much you want to love them again!

Title Author

______________________ ______________________

Why? ______________________________________

______________________ ______________________

Why? ______________________________________

______________________ ______________________

Why? ______________________________________

______________________ ______________________

Why? ______________________________________

______________________ ______________________

Why? ______________________________________

______________________ ______________________

Why? ______________________________________

______________________ ______________________

Why? ______________________________________

READ AGAIN LIST

LIST THE BOOKS YOU LOVED SO MUCH YOU WANT TO LOVE THEM AGAIN!

TITLE AUTHOR

WHY?

WHY?

WHY?

WHY?

WHY?

WHY?

WHY?

RECOMMENDATIONS

Your friend told you all about an incredible book you should read ... what was it called again? Never miss those juicy recs by recording them on the following pages!

Recommendations

Title	Rec'd By	Read?
		☐
		☐
		☐
		☐
		☐
		☐
		☐
		☐
		☐
		☐
		☐
		☐
		☐
		☐
		☐

Recommendations

Title	Rec'd By	Read?
		☐
		☐
		☐
		☐
		☐
		☐
		☐
		☐
		☐
		☐
		☐
		☐
		☐
		☐
		☐

RECOMMENDATIONS

TITLE	REC'D BY	READ?
		☐
		☐
		☐
		☐
		☐
		☐
		☐
		☐
		☐
		☐
		☐
		☐
		☐
		☐
		☐

RECOMMENDATIONS

TITLE	REC'D BY	READ?
		☐
		☐
		☐
		☐
		☐
		☐
		☐
		☐
		☐
		☐
		☐
		☐
		☐
		☐
		☐

Loans In and Out

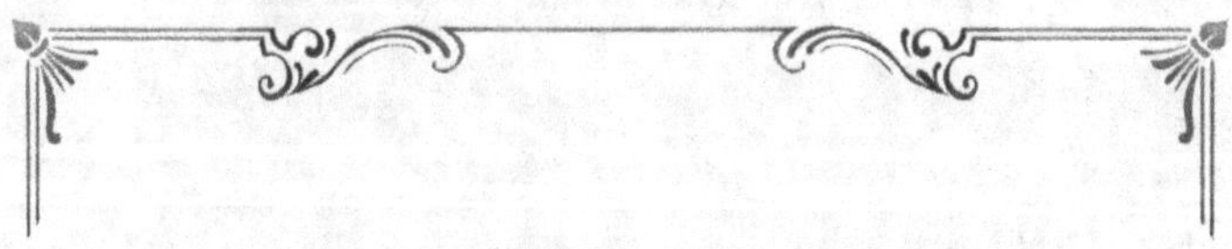

If you and your book besties love to trade tomes, keep track of who has your books, and whose books you need return on the following pages.

Borrowed

Title	From	Returned?

LOANED OUT

BORROWED
TITLE
FROM
RETURNED?

LOANED OUT

TITLE	TO	RETURNED?
		☐
		☐
		☐
		☐
		☐
		☐
		☐
		☐
		☐
		☐
		☐
		☐
		☐
		☐
		☐
		☐
		☐
		☐

Book Reviews and Notes

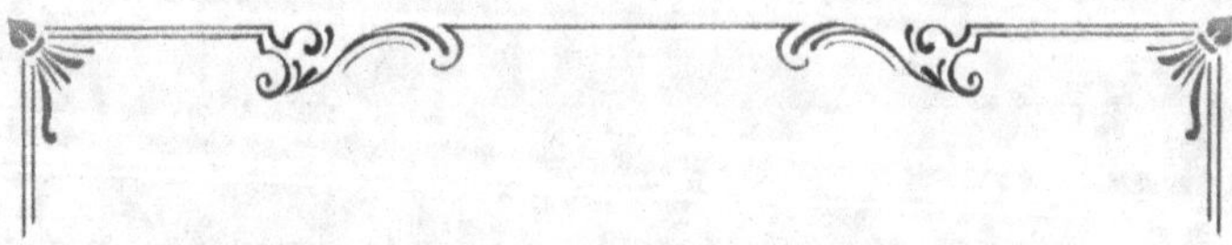

Track your reads! Keep all your notes and thoughts together about the books you've read on the following pages.

Thoughts

Quotes

TITLE

AUTHOR:

GENRE:

☆☆☆☆☆

FORMAT: EBOOK ☐ HARDCOPY ☐ AUDIO ☐

DATE: / / / /

STARTED FINISHED

BOOK LENGTH:

MAIN CHARACTERS:

TROPES:

THE BEST STUFF HAPPENS ON PAGES:

WRITE A REVIEW/LOVE LETTER TO THE AUTHOR?

YES/NO

Thoughts

Quotes

TITLE

____

AUTHOR: ______________________

GENRE: ______________________

☆☆☆☆☆

FORMAT: EBOOK ☐ HARDCOPY ☐ AUDIO ☐

DATE: ____/____/____ ____/____/____

STARTED FINISHED

BOOK LENGTH: ______________________

MAIN CHARACTERS: ______________________

____

TROPES: ______________________

____

THE BEST STUFF HAPPENS ON PAGES:

______ ______ ______ ______

______ ______ ______ ______

WRITE A REVIEW/LOVE LETTER TO THE AUTHOR?

YES/NO

THOUGHTS

QUOTES

TITLE

AUTHOR:

GENRE:

☆☆☆☆☆

FORMAT: EBOOK ☐ HARDCOPY ☐ AUDIO ☐

DATE: / / STARTED / / FINISHED

BOOK LENGTH:

MAIN CHARACTERS:

TROPES:

THE BEST STUFF HAPPENS ON PAGES:

WRITE A REVIEW/LOVE LETTER TO THE AUTHOR?

YES/NO

Thoughts

Quotes

TITLE

____

AUTHOR: ______________________

GENRE: _______________________

☆☆☆☆☆

FORMAT: EBOOK ☐ HARDCOPY ☐ AUDIO ☐

DATE: ____/____/____ ____/____/____
STARTED FINISHED

BOOK LENGTH: __________________

MAIN CHARACTERS: ______________

____

TROPES: ______________________

____

THE BEST STUFF HAPPENS ON PAGES:

______ ______ ______ ______

______ ______ ______ ______

WRITE A REVIEW/LOVE LETTER TO THE AUTHOR?

YES/NO

THOUGHTS

QUOTES

TITLE

AUTHOR:

GENRE:

☆☆☆☆☆

FORMAT: EBOOK ☐ HARDCOPY ☐ AUDIO ☐

DATE: / / / /

STARTED FINISHED

BOOK LENGTH:

MAIN CHARACTERS:

TROPES:

THE BEST STUFF HAPPENS ON PAGES:

WRITE A REVIEW/LOVE LETTER TO THE AUTHOR?

YES/NO

THOUGHTS

QUOTES

TITLE

AUTHOR:

GENRE:

☆☆☆☆☆

FORMAT: EBOOK ☐ HARDCOPY ☐ AUDIO ☐

DATE: / / / /

STARTED FINISHED

BOOK LENGTH:

MAIN CHARACTERS:

TROPES:

THE BEST STUFF HAPPENS ON PAGES:

WRITE A REVIEW/LOVE LETTER TO THE AUTHOR?

YES/NO

THOUGHTS

QUOTES

TITLE

AUTHOR:

GENRE:

☆☆☆☆☆

FORMAT: EBOOK ☐ HARDCOPY ☐ AUDIO ☐

DATE: / / STARTED / / FINISHED

BOOK LENGTH:

MAIN CHARACTERS:

TROPES:

THE BEST STUFF HAPPENS ON PAGES:

WRITE A REVIEW/LOVE LETTER TO THE AUTHOR?

YES/NO

Thoughts

Quotes

TITLE

AUTHOR:

GENRE:

☆☆☆☆☆

FORMAT: EBOOK ☐ HARDCOPY ☐ AUDIO ☐

DATE: / / / /

STARTED FINISHED

BOOK LENGTH:

MAIN CHARACTERS:

TROPES:

THE BEST STUFF HAPPENS ON PAGES:

WRITE A REVIEW/LOVE LETTER TO THE AUTHOR?

YES/NO

Thoughts

Quotes

TITLE

AUTHOR:

GENRE:

☆☆☆☆☆

FORMAT: EBOOK ☐ HARDCOPY ☐ AUDIO ☐

DATE: / / / /

STARTED FINISHED

BOOK LENGTH:

MAIN CHARACTERS:

TROPES:

THE BEST STUFF HAPPENS ON PAGES:

WRITE A REVIEW/LOVE LETTER TO THE AUTHOR?

YES/NO

Thoughts

Quotes

TITLE

AUTHOR:

GENRE:

☆☆☆☆☆

FORMAT: EBOOK ☐ HARDCOPY ☐ AUDIO ☐

DATE: / / / /

STARTED FINISHED

BOOK LENGTH:

MAIN CHARACTERS:

TROPES:

THE BEST STUFF HAPPENS ON PAGES:

WRITE A REVIEW/LOVE LETTER TO THE AUTHOR?

YES/NO

Thoughts

Quotes

TITLE

AUTHOR:

GENRE:

☆☆☆☆☆

FORMAT: EBOOK ☐ HARDCOPY ☐ AUDIO ☐

DATE: / / / /
STARTED FINISHED

BOOK LENGTH:

MAIN CHARACTERS:

TROPES:

THE BEST STUFF HAPPENS ON PAGES:

WRITE A REVIEW/LOVE LETTER TO THE AUTHOR?
YES/NO

THOUGHTS

QUOTES

TITLE

AUTHOR:

GENRE:

☆☆☆☆☆

FORMAT: EBOOK ☐ HARDCOPY ☐ AUDIO ☐

DATE: / / / /

STARTED FINISHED

BOOK LENGTH:

MAIN CHARACTERS:

TROPES:

THE BEST STUFF HAPPENS ON PAGES:

WRITE A REVIEW/LOVE LETTER TO THE AUTHOR?

YES/NO

Thoughts

QUOTES

TITLE

AUTHOR:

GENRE:

☆☆☆☆☆

FORMAT: EBOOK ☐ HARDCOPY ☐ AUDIO ☐

DATE: / / / /

STARTED FINISHED

BOOK LENGTH:

MAIN CHARACTERS:

TROPES:

THE BEST STUFF HAPPENS ON PAGES:

WRITE A REVIEW/LOVE LETTER TO THE AUTHOR?

YES/NO

THOUGHTS

QUOTES

TITLE

AUTHOR:

GENRE:

☆☆☆☆☆

FORMAT: EBOOK ☐ HARDCOPY ☐ AUDIO ☐

DATE: / / STARTED / / FINISHED

BOOK LENGTH:

MAIN CHARACTERS:

TROPES:

THE BEST STUFF HAPPENS ON PAGES:

WRITE A REVIEW/LOVE LETTER TO THE AUTHOR?

YES/NO

THOUGHTS

QUOTES

TITLE

AUTHOR:

GENRE:

☆☆☆☆☆

FORMAT: EBOOK ☐ HARDCOPY ☐ AUDIO ☐

DATE: / / / /

STARTED FINISHED

BOOK LENGTH:

MAIN CHARACTERS:

TROPES:

THE BEST STUFF HAPPENS ON PAGES:

WRITE A REVIEW/LOVE LETTER TO THE AUTHOR?

YES/NO

Thoughts

Quotes

TITLE

AUTHOR:

GENRE:

☆☆☆☆☆

FORMAT: EBOOK ☐ HARDCOPY ☐ AUDIO ☐

DATE: / / / /

STARTED FINISHED

BOOK LENGTH:

MAIN CHARACTERS:

TROPES:

THE BEST STUFF HAPPENS ON PAGES:

WRITE A REVIEW/LOVE LETTER TO THE AUTHOR?

YES/NO

THOUGHTS

QUOTES

TITLE

AUTHOR:

GENRE:

☆☆☆☆☆

FORMAT: EBOOK ☐ HARDCOPY ☐ AUDIO ☐

DATE: / / / /

STARTED FINISHED

BOOK LENGTH:

MAIN CHARACTERS:

TROPES:

THE BEST STUFF HAPPENS ON PAGES:

WRITE A REVIEW/LOVE LETTER TO THE AUTHOR?

YES/NO

Thoughts

Quotes

TITLE

AUTHOR:

GENRE:

☆☆☆☆☆

FORMAT: EBOOK ☐ HARDCOPY ☐ AUDIO ☐

DATE: / / / /

STARTED FINISHED

BOOK LENGTH:

MAIN CHARACTERS:

TROPES:

THE BEST STUFF HAPPENS ON PAGES:

WRITE A REVIEW/LOVE LETTER TO THE AUTHOR?

YES/NO

THOUGHTS

QUOTES

TITLE

____

AUTHOR: ______________________________________

GENRE: _______________________________________

☆☆☆☆☆

FORMAT: EBOOK ☐ HARDCOPY ☐ AUDIO ☐

DATE: ____/____/________ ____/____/________
STARTED FINISHED

BOOK LENGTH: _________________________________

MAIN CHARACTERS: _____________________________

____

TROPES: ______________________________________

____

THE BEST STUFF HAPPENS ON PAGES:

________ ________ ________ ________

________ ________ ________ ________

WRITE A REVIEW/LOVE LETTER TO THE AUTHOR?

YES/NO

THOUGHTS

QUOTES

TITLE

____

AUTHOR: ______________________________

GENRE: ______________________________

☆☆☆☆☆

FORMAT: EBOOK ☐ HARDCOPY ☐ AUDIO ☐

DATE: ____/____/____ (STARTED) ____/____/____ (FINISHED)

BOOK LENGTH: ______________________________

MAIN CHARACTERS: ______________________________

____

TROPES: ______________________________

____

THE BEST STUFF HAPPENS ON PAGES:

______ ______ ______ ______

______ ______ ______ ______

WRITE A REVIEW/LOVE LETTER TO THE AUTHOR?

YES/NO

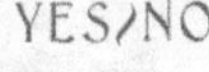

Thoughts

Quotes

TITLE

AUTHOR:

GENRE:

☆☆☆☆☆

FORMAT: EBOOK ☐ HARDCOPY ☐ AUDIO ☐

DATE: / / / /

STARTED FINISHED

BOOK LENGTH:

MAIN CHARACTERS:

TROPES:

THE BEST STUFF HAPPENS ON PAGES:

WRITE A REVIEW/LOVE LETTER TO THE AUTHOR?

YES/NO

Thoughts

Quotes

TITLE

AUTHOR:

GENRE:

☆☆☆☆☆

FORMAT: EBOOK ☐ HARDCOPY ☐ AUDIO ☐

DATE: / / / /

STARTED FINISHED

BOOK LENGTH:

MAIN CHARACTERS:

TROPES:

THE BEST STUFF HAPPENS ON PAGES:

WRITE A REVIEW/LOVE LETTER TO THE AUTHOR?

YES/NO

Thoughts

QUOTES

TITLE

AUTHOR:

GENRE:

☆☆☆☆☆

FORMAT: EBOOK ☐ HARDCOPY ☐ AUDIO ☐

DATE: / / / /

STARTED FINISHED

BOOK LENGTH:

MAIN CHARACTERS:

TROPES:

THE BEST STUFF HAPPENS ON PAGES:

WRITE A REVIEW/LOVE LETTER TO THE AUTHOR?

YES/NO

Thoughts

Quotes

TITLE

AUTHOR:

GENRE:

☆☆☆☆☆

FORMAT: EBOOK ☐ HARDCOPY ☐ AUDIO ☐

DATE: / / / /

STARTED FINISHED

BOOK LENGTH:

MAIN CHARACTERS:

TROPES:

THE BEST STUFF HAPPENS ON PAGES:

WRITE A REVIEW/LOVE LETTER TO THE AUTHOR?

YES/NO

THOUGHTS

QUOTES

TITLE

AUTHOR:

GENRE:

☆☆☆☆☆

FORMAT: EBOOK ☐ HARDCOPY ☐ AUDIO ☐

DATE: / / / /

STARTED FINISHED

BOOK LENGTH:

MAIN CHARACTERS:

TROPES:

THE BEST STUFF HAPPENS ON PAGES:

WRITE A REVIEW/LOVE LETTER TO THE AUTHOR?

YES/NO

Thoughts

Quotes

TITLE

AUTHOR:

GENRE:

☆☆☆☆☆

FORMAT: EBOOK ☐ HARDCOPY ☐ AUDIO ☐

DATE: / / / /

STARTED FINISHED

BOOK LENGTH:

MAIN CHARACTERS:

TROPES:

THE BEST STUFF HAPPENS ON PAGES:

WRITE A REVIEW/LOVE LETTER TO THE AUTHOR?

YES/NO

Thoughts

Quotes

TITLE

____

AUTHOR: ______________________

GENRE: ______________________

☆☆☆☆☆

FORMAT: EBOOK ☐ HARDCOPY ☐ AUDIO ☐

DATE: ____/____/____ ____/____/____
STARTED FINISHED

BOOK LENGTH: ______________________

MAIN CHARACTERS: ______________________

____

TROPES: ______________________

____

THE BEST STUFF HAPPENS ON PAGES:

______ ______ ______ ______

______ ______ ______ ______

WRITE A REVIEW/LOVE LETTER TO THE AUTHOR?

YES/NO

Thoughts

Quotes

TITLE

AUTHOR:

GENRE:

☆☆☆☆☆

FORMAT: EBOOK ☐ HARDCOPY ☐ AUDIO ☐

DATE: / / STARTED / / FINISHED

BOOK LENGTH:

MAIN CHARACTERS:

TROPES:

THE BEST STUFF HAPPENS ON PAGES:

WRITE A REVIEW/LOVE LETTER TO THE AUTHOR?

YES/NO

THOUGHTS

QUOTES

TITLE

AUTHOR:

GENRE:

☆☆☆☆☆

FORMAT: EBOOK ☐ HARDCOPY ☐ AUDIO ☐

DATE: / / / /

STARTED FINISHED

BOOK LENGTH:

MAIN CHARACTERS:

TROPES:

THE BEST STUFF HAPPENS ON PAGES:

WRITE A REVIEW/LOVE LETTER TO THE AUTHOR?

YES/NO

THOUGHTS

QUOTES

TITLE

AUTHOR:

GENRE:

☆☆☆☆☆

FORMAT: EBOOK ☐ HARDCOPY ☐ AUDIO ☐

DATE: / / / /
STARTED FINISHED

BOOK LENGTH:

MAIN CHARACTERS:

TROPES:

THE BEST STUFF HAPPENS ON PAGES:

WRITE A REVIEW/LOVE LETTER TO THE AUTHOR?

YES/NO

Thoughts

Quotes

TITLE

AUTHOR:

GENRE:

☆☆☆☆☆

FORMAT: EBOOK ☐ HARDCOPY ☐ AUDIO ☐

DATE: / / / /

STARTED FINISHED

BOOK LENGTH:

MAIN CHARACTERS:

TROPES:

THE BEST STUFF HAPPENS ON PAGES:

WRITE A REVIEW/LOVE LETTER TO THE AUTHOR?

YES/NO

Thoughts

Quotes

TITLE

AUTHOR:

GENRE:

☆☆☆☆☆

FORMAT: EBOOK ☐ HARDCOPY ☐ AUDIO ☐

DATE: / / / /

STARTED FINISHED

BOOK LENGTH:

MAIN CHARACTERS:

TROPES:

THE BEST STUFF HAPPENS ON PAGES:

WRITE A REVIEW/LOVE LETTER TO THE AUTHOR?

YES/NO

THOUGHTS

QUOTES

TITLE

____

AUTHOR: ______________________

GENRE: ______________________

☆☆☆☆☆

FORMAT: EBOOK ☐ HARDCOPY ☐ AUDIO ☐

DATE: ____/____/____ ____/____/____
STARTED FINISHED

BOOK LENGTH: ______________________

MAIN CHARACTERS: ______________________

____

TROPES: ______________________

____

THE BEST STUFF HAPPENS ON PAGES:

______ ______ ______ ______

______ ______ ______ ______

WRITE A REVIEW/LOVE LETTER TO THE AUTHOR?
YES/NO

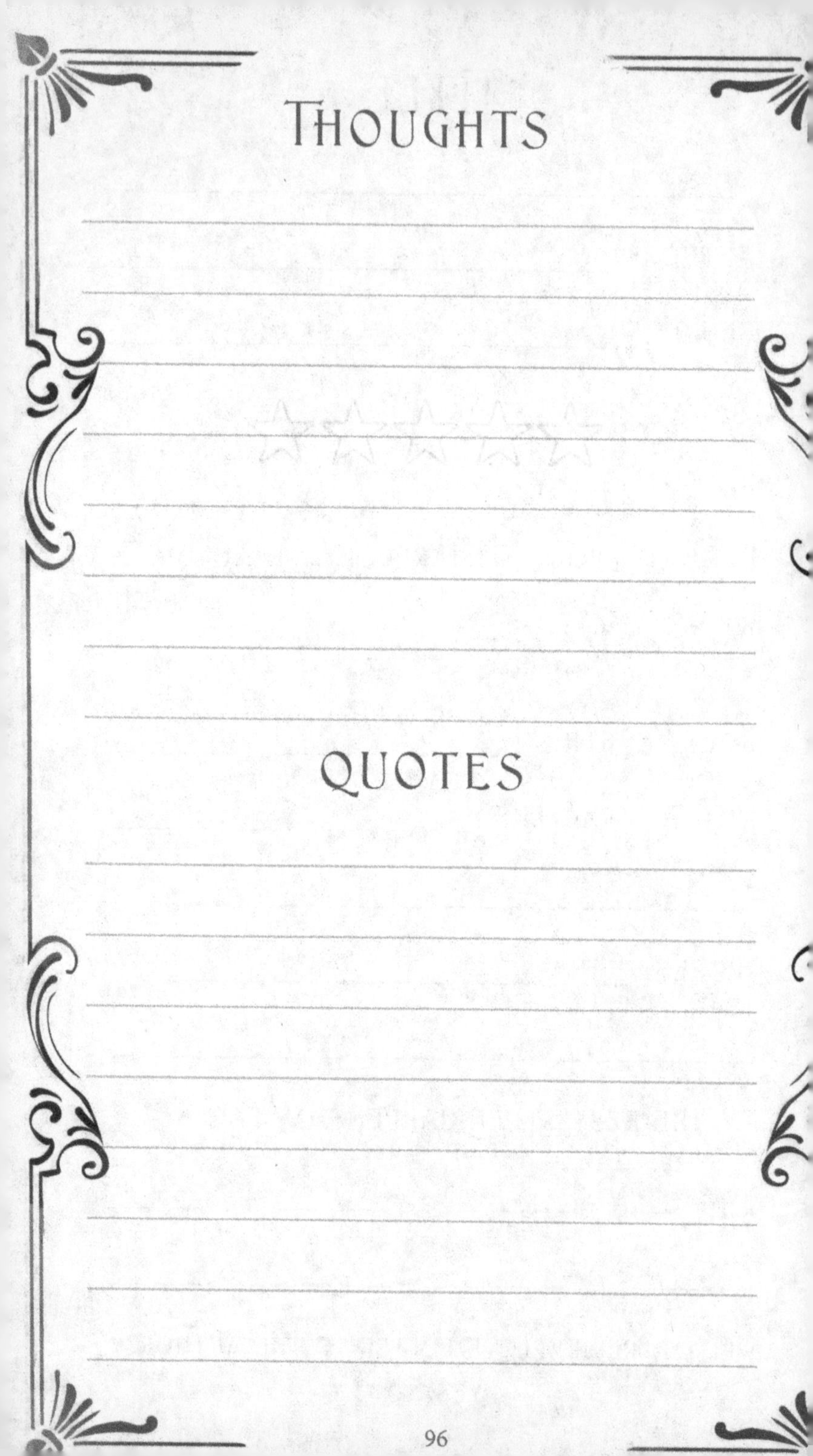

THOUGHTS

QUOTES

TITLE

AUTHOR:

GENRE:

☆☆☆☆☆

FORMAT: EBOOK ☐ HARDCOPY ☐ AUDIO ☐

DATE: / / / /

STARTED FINISHED

BOOK LENGTH:

MAIN CHARACTERS:

TROPES:

THE BEST STUFF HAPPENS ON PAGES:

WRITE A REVIEW/LOVE LETTER TO THE AUTHOR?

YES/NO

THOUGHTS

QUOTES

TITLE

AUTHOR:

GENRE:

☆☆☆☆☆

FORMAT: EBOOK ☐ HARDCOPY ☐ AUDIO ☐

DATE: / / / /

STARTED FINISHED

BOOK LENGTH:

MAIN CHARACTERS:

TROPES:

THE BEST STUFF HAPPENS ON PAGES:

WRITE A REVIEW/LOVE LETTER TO THE AUTHOR?

YES/NO

THOUGHTS

QUOTES

TITLE

AUTHOR:

GENRE:

☆☆☆☆☆

FORMAT: EBOOK ☐ HARDCOPY ☐ AUDIO ☐

DATE: / / / /

STARTED FINISHED

BOOK LENGTH:

MAIN CHARACTERS:

TROPES:

THE BEST STUFF HAPPENS ON PAGES:

WRITE A REVIEW/LOVE LETTER TO THE AUTHOR?

YES/NO

THOUGHTS

QUOTES

TITLE

AUTHOR:

GENRE:

☆☆☆☆☆

FORMAT: EBOOK ☐ HARDCOPY ☐ AUDIO ☐

DATE: / / / /

STARTED FINISHED

BOOK LENGTH:

MAIN CHARACTERS:

TROPES:

THE BEST STUFF HAPPENS ON PAGES:

WRITE A REVIEW/LOVE LETTER TO THE AUTHOR?

YES/NO

THOUGHTS

QUOTES

TITLE

AUTHOR:

GENRE:

☆☆☆☆☆

FORMAT: EBOOK ☐ HARDCOPY ☐ AUDIO ☐

DATE: / / / /

STARTED FINISHED

BOOK LENGTH:

MAIN CHARACTERS:

TROPES:

THE BEST STUFF HAPPENS ON PAGES:

WRITE A REVIEW/LOVE LETTER TO THE AUTHOR?

YES/NO

THOUGHTS

QUOTES

TITLE

AUTHOR:

GENRE:

☆☆☆☆☆

FORMAT: EBOOK ☐ HARDCOPY ☐ AUDIO ☐

DATE: / / / /

STARTED FINISHED

BOOK LENGTH:

MAIN CHARACTERS:

TROPES:

THE BEST STUFF HAPPENS ON PAGES:

WRITE A REVIEW/LOVE LETTER TO THE AUTHOR?

YES/NO

Thoughts

QUOTES

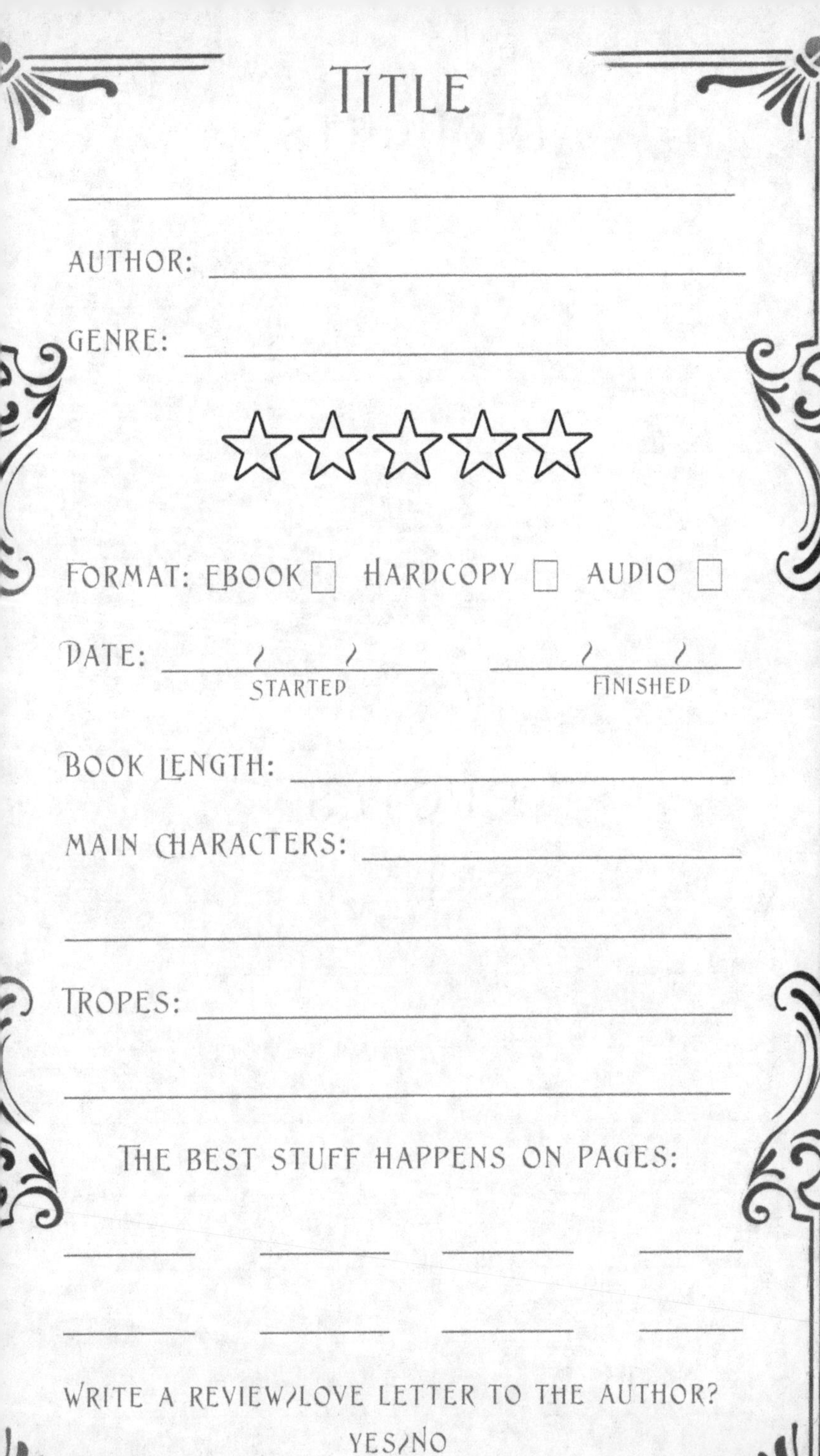

TITLE

AUTHOR:

GENRE:

☆☆☆☆☆

FORMAT: EBOOK ☐ HARDCOPY ☐ AUDIO ☐

DATE: / / — / /
STARTED FINISHED

BOOK LENGTH:

MAIN CHARACTERS:

TROPES:

THE BEST STUFF HAPPENS ON PAGES:

WRITE A REVIEW/LOVE LETTER TO THE AUTHOR?
YES/NO

THOUGHTS

QUOTES

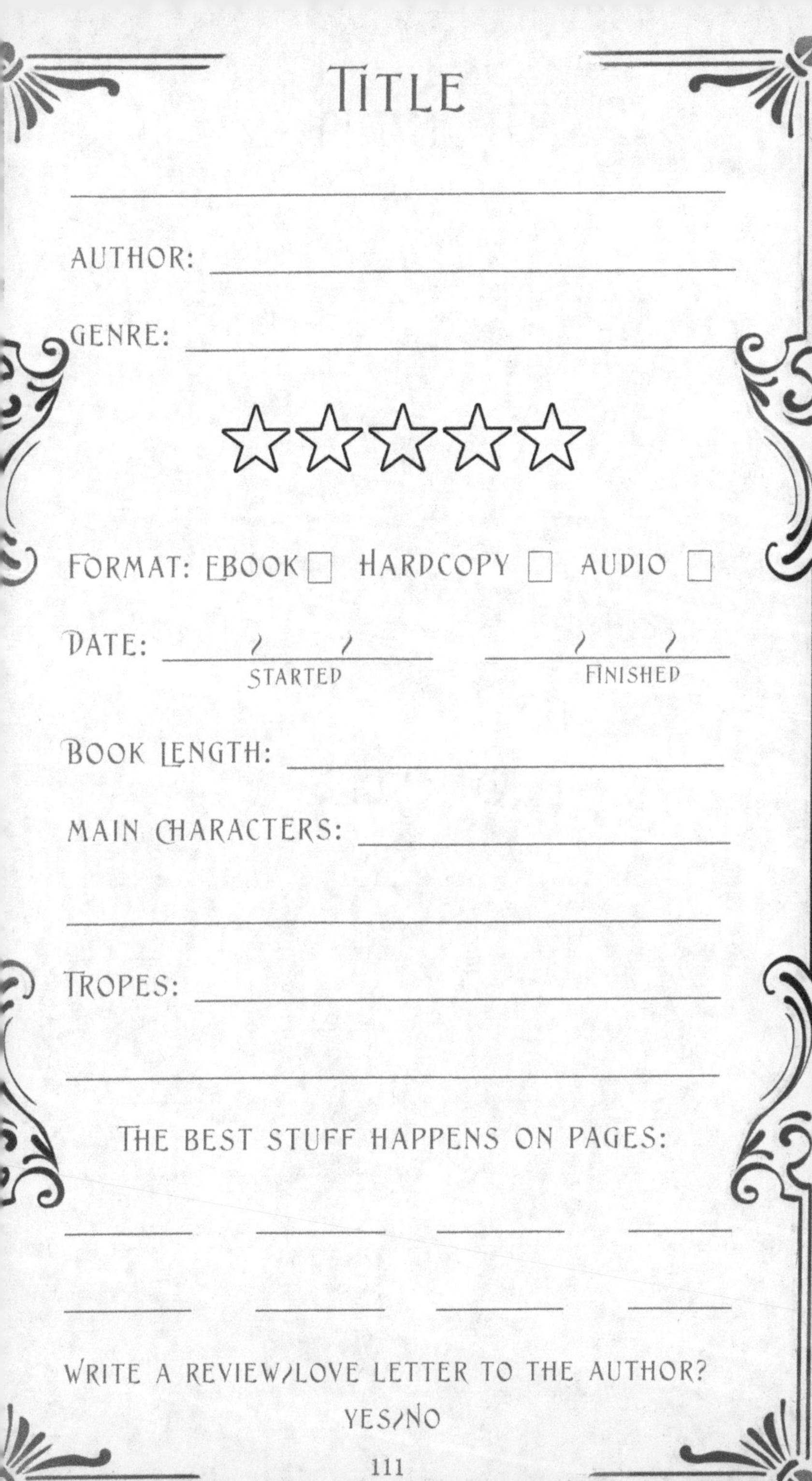

TITLE

AUTHOR:

GENRE:

☆☆☆☆☆

FORMAT: EBOOK ☐ HARDCOPY ☐ AUDIO ☐

DATE: / / STARTED / / FINISHED

BOOK LENGTH:

MAIN CHARACTERS:

TROPES:

THE BEST STUFF HAPPENS ON PAGES:

WRITE A REVIEW/LOVE LETTER TO THE AUTHOR?

YES/NO

THOUGHTS

QUOTES

TITLE

____

AUTHOR: ______________________

GENRE: ______________________

☆☆☆☆☆

FORMAT: EBOOK ☐ HARDCOPY ☐ AUDIO ☐

DATE: ____/____/____ ____/____/____
STARTED FINISHED

BOOK LENGTH: ______________________

MAIN CHARACTERS: ______________________

____

TROPES: ______________________

____

THE BEST STUFF HAPPENS ON PAGES:

______ ______ ______ ______

______ ______ ______ ______

WRITE A REVIEW/LOVE LETTER TO THE AUTHOR?
YES/NO

Thoughts

Quotes

TITLE

AUTHOR:

GENRE:

☆☆☆☆☆

FORMAT: EBOOK ☐ HARDCOPY ☐ AUDIO ☐

DATE: / / / /

STARTED FINISHED

BOOK LENGTH:

MAIN CHARACTERS:

TROPES:

THE BEST STUFF HAPPENS ON PAGES:

WRITE A REVIEW/LOVE LETTER TO THE AUTHOR?

YES/NO

THOUGHTS

QUOTES

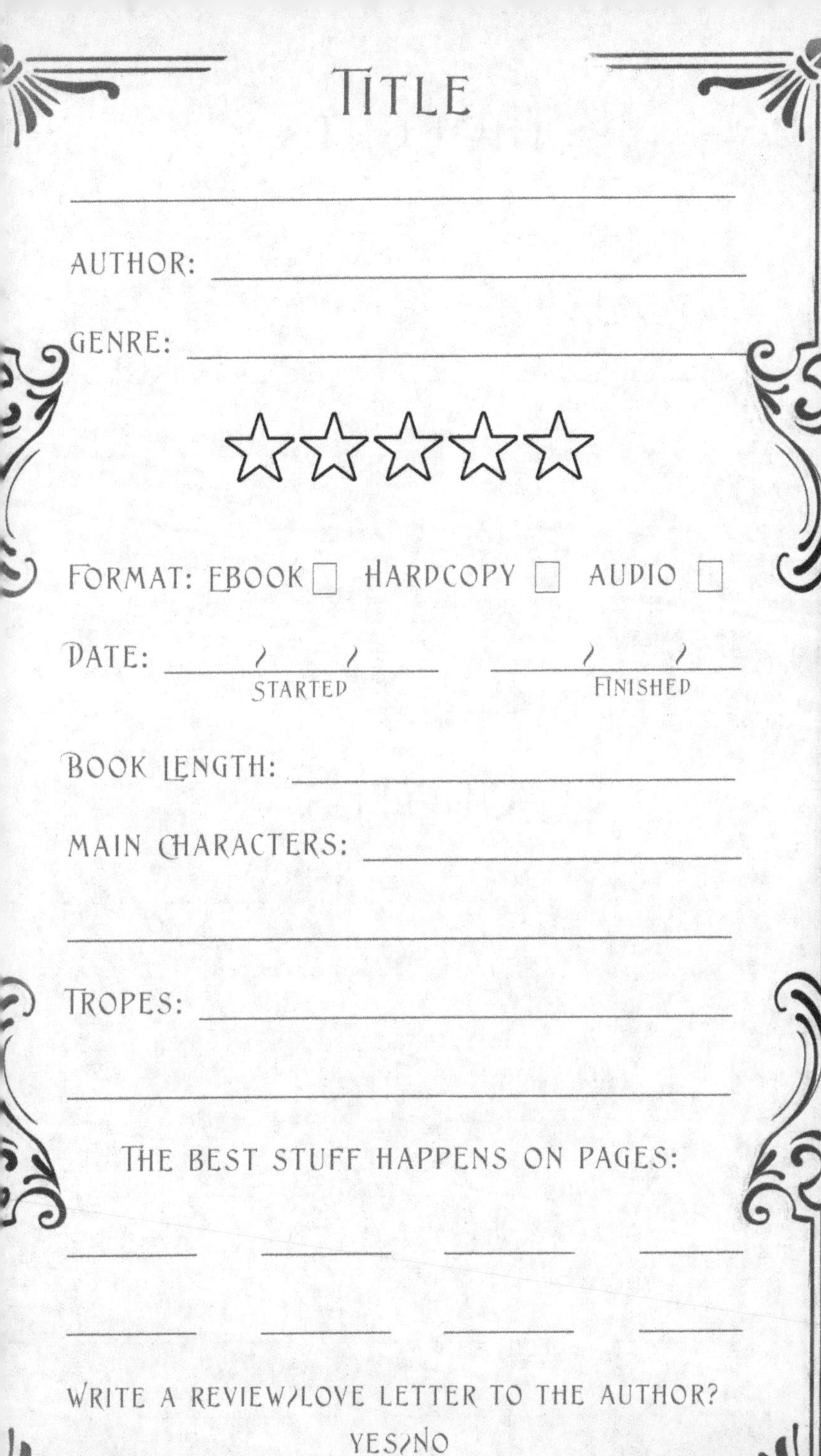

TITLE

AUTHOR:

GENRE:

☆☆☆☆☆

FORMAT: EBOOK ☐ HARDCOPY ☐ AUDIO ☐

DATE: / / STARTED / / FINISHED

BOOK LENGTH:

MAIN CHARACTERS:

TROPES:

THE BEST STUFF HAPPENS ON PAGES:

WRITE A REVIEW/LOVE LETTER TO THE AUTHOR?

YES/NO

THOUGHTS

QUOTES

TITLE

AUTHOR:

GENRE:

☆☆☆☆☆

FORMAT: EBOOK ☐ HARDCOPY ☐ AUDIO ☐

DATE: / / / /

STARTED FINISHED

BOOK LENGTH:

MAIN CHARACTERS:

TROPES:

THE BEST STUFF HAPPENS ON PAGES:

WRITE A REVIEW/LOVE LETTER TO THE AUTHOR?

YES/NO

Thoughts

Quotes

TITLE

AUTHOR:

GENRE:

☆☆☆☆☆

FORMAT: EBOOK ☐ HARDCOPY ☐ AUDIO ☐

DATE: / / / /

STARTED FINISHED

BOOK LENGTH:

MAIN CHARACTERS:

TROPES:

THE BEST STUFF HAPPENS ON PAGES:

WRITE A REVIEW/LOVE LETTER TO THE AUTHOR?

YES/NO

Thoughts

Quotes

TITLE

AUTHOR:

GENRE:

☆☆☆☆☆

FORMAT: EBOOK ☐ HARDCOPY ☐ AUDIO ☐

DATE: / / / /

STARTED FINISHED

BOOK LENGTH:

MAIN CHARACTERS:

TROPES:

THE BEST STUFF HAPPENS ON PAGES:

WRITE A REVIEW/LOVE LETTER TO THE AUTHOR?

YES/NO

Thoughts

Quotes

TITLE

____

AUTHOR: __________________________

GENRE: ___________________________

☆☆☆☆☆

FORMAT: EBOOK ☐ HARDCOPY ☐ AUDIO ☐

DATE: ____/____/____ ____/____/____

STARTED FINISHED

BOOK LENGTH: ______________________

MAIN CHARACTERS: ___________________

____

TROPES: ___________________________

____

THE BEST STUFF HAPPENS ON PAGES:

______ ______ ______ ______

______ ______ ______ ______

WRITE A REVIEW/LOVE LETTER TO THE AUTHOR?

YES/NO

Thoughts

Quotes

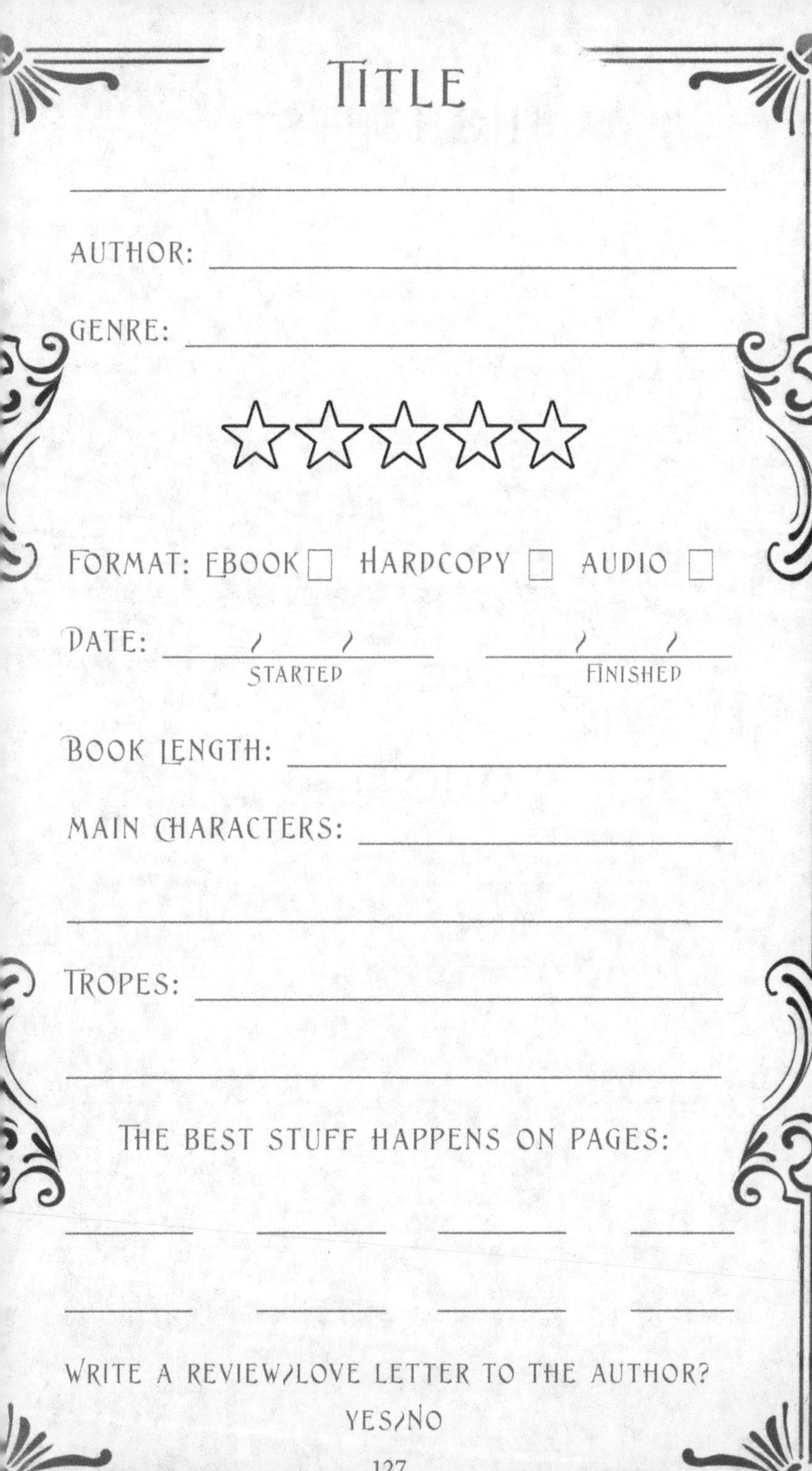

TITLE

AUTHOR:

GENRE:

☆☆☆☆☆

FORMAT: EBOOK ☐ HARDCOPY ☐ AUDIO ☐

DATE: / / / /

STARTED FINISHED

BOOK LENGTH:

MAIN CHARACTERS:

TROPES:

THE BEST STUFF HAPPENS ON PAGES:

WRITE A REVIEW/LOVE LETTER TO THE AUTHOR?

YES/NO

THOUGHTS

QUOTES

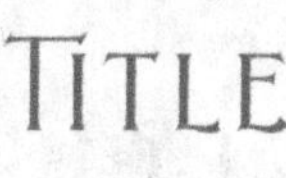

AUTHOR: ______________________

GENRE: ______________________

☆☆☆☆☆

FORMAT: EBOOK ☐ HARDCOPY ☐ AUDIO ☐

DATE: ____/____/____ ____/____/____
STARTED FINISHED

BOOK LENGTH: ______________________

MAIN CHARACTERS: ______________________

____

TROPES: ______________________

____

THE BEST STUFF HAPPENS ON PAGES:

______ ______ ______ ______

______ ______ ______ ______

WRITE A REVIEW/LOVE LETTER TO THE AUTHOR?
YES/NO

THOUGHTS

QUOTES

TITLE

AUTHOR:

GENRE:

☆☆☆☆☆

FORMAT: EBOOK ☐ HARDCOPY ☐ AUDIO ☐

DATE: / / / /

STARTED FINISHED

BOOK LENGTH:

MAIN CHARACTERS:

TROPES:

THE BEST STUFF HAPPENS ON PAGES:

WRITE A REVIEW/LOVE LETTER TO THE AUTHOR?

YES/NO

ORACLE DECKS

ORACLE OF THE MERMAIDS AND WILD WISDOM OF THE FAERY ORACLE

WRITTEN BY LUCY CAVENDISH - ARTWORK BY SELINA FENECH

PRACTICAL MAGIC ORACLE DECK

WRITTEN BY SERENE CONNEELEY - ARTWORK BY SELINA FENECH

SELINA'S ART ALSO APPEARS IN THESE MULTI ARTIST DECKS-

www.blueangelonline.com www.78tarot.cards

ABOUT SELINA FENECH

As a lover of all things fantasy, Selina has made a living as an artist for over 15 years selling her magical creations. Her works range from oil paintings to oracle decks, dolls to digital scrapbooking, plus Young Adult novels, jewelry, figurines, and colouring books.

Selina lives in Australia and loves food, gardening, geekery, and all things fantasy. Selina's mission in life is to share magic and enchant hearts through her art and words.

Selina's art is available as figurines, device cases, doll patterns, fabric, cross stitch, art books and much, much more.

Discover a world of fantasy at www.selinafenech.com

Need More Books?

Beshadowed - Urban Fantasy

You have been lied to. Werewolves, vampires, ghosts … they aren't what you think. What is really lurking in the dark? ***Monster hunters, mysteries, light horror, and slow burn romance.***

COMPLETE SERIES!

Shadow Dragon Saga - Young Adult Epic Fantas

Into a haunted realm, a creature unlike any is born, and must be protected. ***Young adult fantasy with diverse cast, enemies to lovers, dragons, and magic.***

Heartsblood - Vampire Romance

Her blood is irresistible, but is it worth the cost? A struggling actress fights for her freedom against the ravenous undead. ***Adventure, suspense, and a happily ever after romance with spice.***

COMPLETE SERIES!

EBOOKS - PAPERBACKS - HARDCOVERS - AUDIOBOOKS

FAIRY TALE REALMS - YA FAIRY TALE RETELLINGS

What if Rumpelstiltskin was a ghost haunting a cruel billionaire's estate?
What if Cinderella had to discover who was trying to assassinate the king?

Mysteries with sweet romance and diverse characters. Happily Ever After Standalone Novels.

MEMORY'S WAKE - ILLUSTRATED YA PORTAL FANTASY

A modern goth teen is lost and hunted in a dangerous fairytale world.
Arthurian lore/Victorian era, royalty, fae, dragons, and magic.

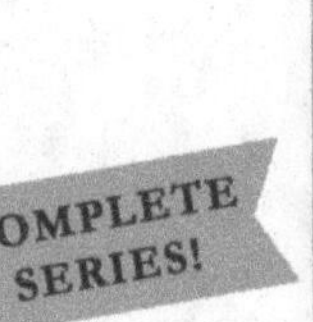

EMPATH CHRONICLES - YOUNG ADULT SUPERHERO ROMANCE

Overwhelming teenage emotions can be deadly when they grant superpowers.
Action and adventure, good vs evil, sweet romance and wholesome friendships.

Cut out the bookmark to keep your place within your reading journal!

Cut out the bookmark to keep your place within you reading journal!

Printed in the USA
CPSIA information can be obtained
at www.ICGtesting.com
LVHW030901171124
796857LV00018B/786

* 9 7 8 1 9 2 2 3 9 0 8 4 4 *